GREAT EXPLORATIONS

SIR FRANCIS DRAKE

Navigator and Pirate

EARLE RICE, JR.

BENCHMARK BOOKS

MARSHALL CAVENDISH
NEW YORK

With special thanks to Steven Pitti, Yale University, and Paul Mapp, The College of William and Mary, for their careful reading of this manuscript.

Benchmark Books
Marshall Cavendish
99 White Plains Road
Tarrytown, New York 10591-9001
www.marshallcavendish.com

Library of Congress Cataloging-in-Publication Data

Rice, Earle.
Sir Francis Drake: navigator and pirate / by Earle Rice, Jr.
p. cm. — (Great explorations)
Summary: A biography of the sixteenth-century English explorer who became a national hero for sailing around the world, and confirmed that status through his service as a Vice Admiral battling the Spanish Armada.
ISBN 0-7614-1483-5
1. Drake, Francis, Sir, 1540?-1596—Juvenile literature. 2. Great Britain—History, Naval—Tudors, 1485-1603—Juvenile literature. 3. Great Britain—History—Elizabeth, 1558-1603—Biography—Juvenile literature. 4. America—Discovery and exploration—English—Juvenile literature. 5. Explorers—Great Britain—Biography—Juvenile literature. 6. Privateering—History—16th century—Juvenile literature. 7. Admirals—Great Britain—Biography—Juvenile literature. [1. Drake, Francis, Sir, 1540?-1596. 2. Great Britain—History, Naval—Tudors, 1485-1603. 3. Great Britain—History—Elizabeth, 1558-1603. 4. Explorers. 5. Admirals. 6. Voyages around the world.] I. Title. II. Series.
DA86.22.D7 R53 2002
942.05'5'092—dc21

2002003523

Photo Research by Candlepants Incorporated
Cover Photo: The Bridgeman Art Library / Private Collection / Christie's Images
Cover Inset: Art Resource, NY / Victoria and Albert Museum, London

The photographs in this book are used by permission and through the courtesy of; *Corbis* : 21, 35; Bettmann, 5, 9, 15, 23, 25, 44, 55, 65; Archivo Iconographico, S.A., 6, 17, 26, 45; Bob Krist, 7; Stapleton Collection, 12, 16; Arne Hodalic, 32; Historical Picture Archive, 42; Baldwin H. Ward and Kathryn C. Ward, 48. *The Bridgman Art Library*: Private Collection / Ken Welsh, 10; Royal Geographic Society, London, UK, 18; Private Collection, 39; Private Collection, 49; Christie's Images, London, UK, 57; Private Collection / The Stapleton Collection, 60-61. *Art Resource, NY*: 13; Eric Lessing, 63. *The Art Archive*: Cornelis de Vries, 37; Eileen Tweedy, 59.

Printed in Hong Kong

1   3   5   6   4   2

Contents

foreword

Few fictional stories of high adventure and daring can match the rousing, provocative, real-life story of Francis Drake—slave trader, privateer, pirate, expert navigator, fighting admiral, and the first Englishman to circumnavigate the globe. Born with the scent of the sea in his nose and the glint of gold in his eye, Drake set out at a young age to seek fame and fortune on the great oceans of the world.

Drake rose swiftly from apprentice seaman in England's coastal waters to master mariner in the four corners of the world. His exploits and seamanship soon earned him the admiration of the English and the enmity of their enemies abroad. By 1572, his attacks against Spanish treasure ships and New World settlements in the Caribbean had established him among Spaniards as the most feared and hated predator on the Spanish Main, that is, the north coast of South America, from the Isthmus of Panama to the delta of the Orinoco River. They called him *El Draque*—the Dragon.

Sir Francis Drake—shown here greeting an Eastern prince—explored many parts of the world previously unknown to Europeans.

In 1577, Drake embarked on his famous around-the-world voyage. He sailed through the Strait of Magellan and robbed Spanish vessels and settlements along the west coast of South America. Arguably, he landed briefly in what is now California, where many believe he claimed the land for England. The intrepid sea captain then piloted his tiny ship, the *Golden Hind*, across the Pacific, navigated through the East Indies, and rounded the Cape of Good Hope. When he finally returned home, almost three years later, he sailed into the English port of Plymouth loaded with Spanish gold, silver and other riches. Elizabeth I, England's queen, knighted Drake for his extraordinary voyage—and for a share of the treasure.

The now Sir Francis Drake continued to plague the much-despised Spaniards for another fifteen years. Spain was England's greatest rival for control of the seas. Moreover, Queen Elizabeth I had restored England to Protestantism; Philip II of Spain championed a return to Catholicism. A clash between the two European powers seemed all but inevitable. When war with Spain approached in 1587, Elizabeth called upon Drake to raid a Spanish fleet which was gathering in Cadiz for an assault on England. Drake delivered.

This sixteenth-century map shows the world as the people of Drake's time knew it.

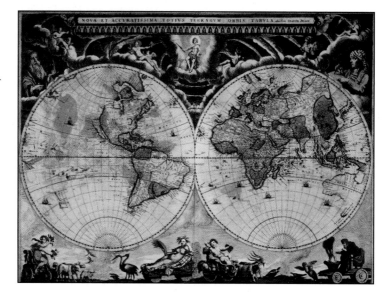

In 36 hours, with a fleet of 23 vessels and 2,100 seamen, he destroyed nearly two dozen Spanish ships and tons of supplies destined for the Spanish Armada, Spain's great navy. Later, when the Armada loomed off England's shores in 1588, Drake, now a vice admiral in Queen Elizabeth's navy, sailed from Plymouth to play a key role in routing and ultimately defeating the Spaniards.

Seven years later, Drake answered one final call from his queen. In 1595, he sailed once again for the Caribbean and engaged in another campaign against Spanish holdings. The voyage failed—largely because his fleet fell victim to disease—and Drake did not return from it.

Today, in Plymouth—a seaport of a quarter-million people—a larger-than-life bronze statue of Sir Francis Drake dominates the Hoe, the city's southern waterfront. More than four centuries after Drake's death, his sculpted image gazes eternally seaward.

A statue in Plymouth, England, honoring Sir Francis Drake, the seaport's most famous resident

Few men live lives that exceed their dreams. Sir Francis Drake was one who did. This is his story—blemishes and all.

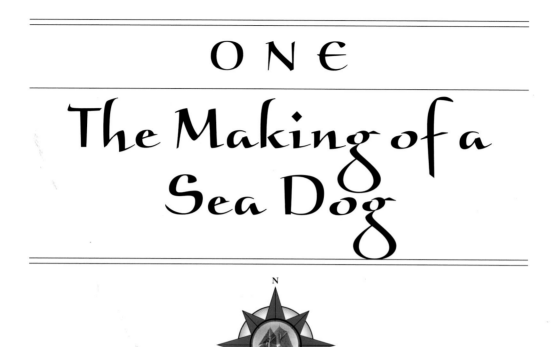

ONE

The Making of a Sea Dog

Francis Drake was born at Crowndale, a farm located about a mile southwest of the town and abbey of Tavistock, Devon, in England's heathery hill country. No one knows the exact date of his birth. Speculations range anywhere from 1538 to 1546. Harry Kelsey, a recent biographer, writes, "Francis Drake, by the best estimate, was born in February or March 1540." In any event, Francis entered life as the first of twelve children born to Edmund Drake, a farmer, and his spouse, possibly (though it is unverifiable) the former Anna Myllwaye.

Drake's father is thought to have been a seafaring man before marrying and settling down to a farmer's life. Edmund may have influenced his eldest son's attraction to the sea at an early age. But religion likely influenced the future of young Francis even more.

Francis was born in a time of religious conflict in England and throughout Europe called the Protestant Reformation. In 1520, Martin

Sir Francis Drake—sailor, slave trader, explorer, and pirate

The Protestant reformer Martin Luther burns a papal edict. This defiant act sparked centuries of religious conflict—and shaped the young Francis Drake's view of the world.

Luther, a German monk, had broken with the Roman Catholic Church, denouncing it as corrupt and mercenary and calling for reforms. Protestantism had soon become common among English seamen. A generation later, a pro-Catholic uprising in southwest England in 1549 forced Edmund Drake, a free-spoken Protestant, to move his family eastward, to Chatham, Kent, to avoid religious persecution.

Nearly penniless but ever-resourceful, the Drakes took up residence in one of the abandoned warships moored near the Royal Navy's main base at Chatham, on the south bank of the river Medway. The half-built warships were the remnants of King Henry VIII's efforts to build a navy a decade earlier. Drake's father acquired their new residence in exchange for the family's former country cottage home.

Edmund, a literate man and devout Protestant, supported his family by reading the Bible to uneducated sailors and shipbuilders in Chatham. Young Francis never attended school but learned to read and write at his father's knee. In later years he would speak eloquently and persuasively, enabling him to win many skeptics over to his point of view. Edmund also instilled in his eldest son a deep reverence for God and an equally ingrained hatred of Catholics, whom Francis called "enemies of God."

Preaching soon proved an insufficient way to provide for a growing family, and Francis was forced to go to sea while he was still a boy. His father apprenticed him to a small coastal vessel that sailed from port to port in the North Sea, one of the harshest stretches of water in the world. This unforgiving environment challenged Francis to the limits of his abilities. But he learned invaluable lessons in the art of seamanship—lessons that would later serve him well. Francis met every challenge and in no time earned the right to be called a "sea dog," that is, a seasoned sailor.

A few years later, Francis's vessel's owner—an heirless bachelor—died and left him the little ship. Francis Drake was now a sea captain and master of his own ship. Sailing the North Sea with an overloaded vessel—navigating by the stars and compass, often avoiding sandbars and rocky coastlines at risk to limb or life—rewarded the young sea dog with a sizeable profit. Hauling coal and timber across the English Channel to France and the Netherlands, coupled with his thrifty nature, enabled him to put aside "a pretty sum of money." Yet his adventurous spirit soon became bored with the repetition and limits of his coastal trade route.

The years at sea had by then formed the character and filled out the frame of this short, stocky, powerfully built young man with reddish brown hair and a cheerful expression. Motivated by ambition, a desire for adventure, and perhaps a bit of greed, Francis Drake set his blue eyes on far horizons. When he was about twenty-three years old, he sold his ship and went to Plymouth, where he joined the fleet of John Hawkins, a distant relative.

John Hawkins—usually defined as Drake's cousin, although the exact relationship is not clear—was a member of a wealthy family of

John Hawkins introduced his kinsman Francis Drake to the slave trade—and to piracy.

Millions of Africans were forced into slavery to supply labor for Europe's colonies in the New World.

merchant shipowners. History also gives him the notorious credit for founding the English slave trade. Dealing in slaves did not then inspire the contempt that it justifiably does today. Despicable as it was to treat Africans and others as less than human beings, many Europeans regarded slaving as just another way of turning a profit. About a decade older than Drake, Hawkins had made successful slaving voyages in 1562 and 1564, referring to his cargo as "our Negroes and our other merchandise."

Hawkins sent Drake on a slave-trading voyage to the west coast of Africa and across the Atlantic to the Spanish Main. Drake served aboard the 180-ton *Swallow* as a purser—the ship's paymaster and record-keeper—under Captain John Lovell. Drake's first venture on the open sea was a financial failure. His next voyage to the Americas was to end in disaster.

T W O

Drake's War

By the end of the fifteenth century, the European states of Portugal and Spain had acquired both the will and the means—daring men and sturdy ships—for far-ranging explorations at sea. After the voyages of Christopher Columbus and the discovery of the so-called New World in the Western Hemisphere, Portuguese and Spanish mariners sailed the oceans to trade, loot, conquer, and, increasingly, to spread religion.

The Portuguese were quick to exploit commercial opportunities in new lands both to the west and to the east. Portugal claimed Brazil in 1500, Mauritius in 1505, Malacca in 1509, and the Spice Islands (Indonesia) in 1511. Spain soon took the lead in exploiting the New World, settling Cuba in 1511 and using it as a base for further acquisitions in the west. In 1519 and 1520, Hernando Cortés seized what is now Mexico. During the next two decades, his countrymen established

The Spanish conquistadores—such as Hernando Cortés, shown here meeting the Aztec emperor Montezuma—ravaged the New World in their search for riches.

permanent settlements in what are now Costa Rica, Honduras, Guatemala, Colombia, Venezuela, and Peru.

The discovery of gold in the new lands claimed by the Spaniards signaled the beginning of Spain's Golden Age. Enormous quantities of gold and silver from the colonies flowed into Spain over the next several decades. By the mid-1500s, Spain stood unrivaled as the most powerful country in the world.

In the early days, oppressive Spanish *conquistadors* (conquerors) and colonizers stripped the local populations of long-accumulated treasures— gold, silver, art objects, gems, and so on—and sent the loot to Spain.

Later, the conquerors forced the conquered to labor in the gold and silver mines of New Spain (Mexico) and those of what are now Peru and Bolivia. Entire native populations were extinguished by hard labor—literally worked to death—by other inhumane treatment, and by disease.

Friar Bartolomé de las Casas, the first priest to be ordained in the New World, suggested that Spanish colonists might substitute Africans for native labor in the mines and plantations of the Americas. After witnessing countless cruelties and degradations inflicted upon the Africans by Spanish slave owners, the friar lived to regret his suggestion. By then, however, the slave trade had become a flourishing enterprise that would thrive for more than three hundred years. The greed that

Hernando Cortés, Spanish conqueror of Mexico

motivated men to enslave and mistreat their fellow human beings knew no class distinctions or national boundaries. And John Hawkins, Frances Drake, and many other Elizabethan sea dogs gave in willingly to the lure of slave-trading riches.

When Francis Drake returned to Plymouth in September 1567, he found John Hawkins ready to begin another slaving expedition to the Caribbean. Hawkins had assembled six ships for the voyage, which he hoped would open the Spanish Indies to the English slave trade. London investors backed the venture. The queen herself furnished two of the Royal Navy's warships—the 700-ton, 26-gun *Jesus of Lubeck* and the 300-ton, 24-gun *Minion*.

Queen Elizabeth I, shown here in a sixteenth-century portrait, was one of England's greatest rulers.

ELISABETHA REG: ANGLIÆ.

Pirates attack a Spanish galleon.

English sailors had lagged behind Spanish navigators in overseas explorations in the first half of the sixteenth century. By the 1560s, however, they had begun awakening to the prospect of the great wealth to be gained in the New World. And too, Elizabeth I was concerned by the threat posed to England by the growing might of Spain and the worsening relations between the two nations. Although she refused to accept the legitimacy of Spain's claim to a monopoly in the Americas, she dared not risk open warfare with Philip II's superior forces.

Secretly, she condoned English privateering raids—raids conducted by armed, privately owned vessels commanded by private persons and commissioned by a government to act against a hostile nation. Elizabeth particularly approved such raids against Spanish shipping and ports and used the Crown's share of the booty—usually 10 percent—to support royal revenues and rebuild the Royal Navy. Spain's navy and merchant fleet dominated the seas and the sea lanes leading to riches in the New World. When ready, Elizabeth intended to compete with Spain for mastery of the seas—until the day when Britain would rule the waves. Under Elizabeth I, the British Empire began its slow rise.

On his earlier voyages to the Caribbean, Hawkins himself had demonstrated that Spain's trade monopoly in the New World could be successfully breached. When word of his latest voyage reached the Spanish embassy in London, Spain's ambassador protested to the queen. Elizabeth assured him that Hawkins would violate no Spanish law. Skeptical, the ambassador dispatched an urgent warning to the king of Spain.

Hawkins selected the *Jesus of Lubeck* as his flagship and appointed Francis Drake as one of the ship's officers. The tiny fleet of six ships departed Plymouth in October 1567 and set a course for the "Slave Coast," the West African coast from Cape Verde to Sierra Leone. Overcoming numerous setbacks—storms at sea and disease ashore in Africa—the Hawkins party finally secured about five hundred Africans, most of them through negotiations with African chieftains, others by kidnapping. Their total included fifty unsold slaves left over from Lovell's voyage and a few more seized from three Portuguese vessels captured off the African coast. Hawkins added the captured vessels to his fleet and gave command of the *Gratia Dei* (Grace of God) to Francis. The English fleet—now with nine ships—set course for the Spanish Main on February 2, 1568.

The Hawkins expedition reached Borburata, on the Venezuelan coast, seven weeks later. They soon found that instructions from the king of Spain had preceded them, threatening the success of their venture. As one sailor's account puts it, "We coasted from place to place making our traffic with the Spaniards as we might, somewhat hardly, because the King had straitly commanded all his governors in those parts by no means to suffer trade with us." Undeterred, Hawkins combined diplomacy and force to sell his cargo.

Hawkins intimidated Spanish officials at Borburata with the size of his fleet, and they agreed to trade with him. Just before the entire fleet departed Borburata in late May, Hawkins sent Drake ahead with two of the smaller ships. Drake sailed westward, now in command of the fifty-ton *Judith* and the thirty-three-ton *Angel*, to Rio de la Hacha, their next port of call. A year earlier, the colonists at Rio de la Hacha had resisted John Lovell's effort to trade by force, and Lovell had returned to England with unsold slaves. Now the Spaniards greeted Drake with cannon fire. Drake answered by putting a cannonball through the house of the local governor, Miguel de Castellanos, and blockading the port.

Hawkins arrived with the rest of his fleet on June 10. When Castellanos failed to meet his demands for permission to trade, Hawkins landed with his band of slave-traders-turned-pirates and ravaged the town. The colonists finally agreed to buy two hundred slaves and paid a handsome ransom to keep the raiders from destroying the town. Hawkins and his "traders" sailed next for Santa Marta, where he sold about 110 slaves to colonists in desperate need of laborers. Farther west, at the more heavily defended port of Cartagena, the Spaniards drove back the English pirates.

In mid-August, with the hurricane season well advanced and eight of his ships carrying enough gold, silver, and pearls for a profitable voyage, Hawkins decided to head for home with a smaller fleet. Abandoning one of the Portuguese vessels at Cartagena, he sailed north with eight ships, setting course for the Yucatan Channel and the Straits of Florida. Just beyond Cabo San Antonio, a raging storm struck the Eng-

A nineteenth-century view of the harbor at San Juan de Ulúa

lish ships and scattered them every which way. The 150-ton *William and John* became separated from the others and eventually made it home alone. Most of the remaining seven ships sustained severe damages, including Hawkins's flagship, the *Jesus of Lubeck*. Hawkins and his captains were driven to seek repairs in San Juan de Ulúa, the fortified port of Veracruz, in what is now Mexico.

San Juan de Ulúa was one of two ports in the New World—the other being Nombre de Dios on the Isthmus of Panama—that Spanish flotas visited annually. Flotas were convoys of merchant ships escorted by warships. On outward voyages, they carried a year's supply of food, clothing, and other essential provisions to the colonies. On return trips, they hauled from the Americas the gold, silver, and precious gems that formed the essence of Spain's wealth and power.

As chance would have it, Hawkins and his storm-buffeted fleet entered the harbor at San Juan de Ulúa only a few days before the arrival of the annual flota. Hawkins and his men easily secured the fort at the mouth of the bay and began bargaining for permission to repair their vessels from a position of strength. All went well until the flota showed up with two warships and eleven merchant vessels. Hawkins found himself negotiating with the newly appointed viceroy of New Spain, Martín Enríquez.

Hawkins controlled the harbor entrance and stood in a position to prevent the Spaniards from entering the port. Francis Drake saw the flota's arrival as an opportunity to strike a blow against Spain. But Hawkins, fearing that an act of war on his part would upset the queen, only wanted assurance from Enríquez that his own ships would not be attacked if he permitted the flota to enter. Accordingly, he sent a message to the viceroy "giving him to understand that before I would suffer them to enter the port, there would be some order of conditions pass between us, for our safe-being there, and maintenance of peace." Enríquez agreed but held not the slightest intention of standing by his agreement.

A few days later, the viceroy ordered an attack on the English ships and a full-scale battle erupted. During the bitter fighting the Spaniards lost two galleons (warships). On the other side, only the *Judith* and *Minion* survived the battle. Drake and Hawkins made their separate escapes—Drake fled aboard the *Judith*, Hawkins aboard the *Minion*. The Spaniards captured or sank the remaining English ships.

Drake's homeward voyage proved uneventful, but Hawkins returned to Plymouth with only fifteen survivors. An acute shortage of food and water forced a hundred of his crew to plead with him to be put ashore on the coast of New Spain. Many of them died from sickness and malnutrition. Others surrendered to the Spaniards, who executed two of them. The rest received two hundred lashes and sentences of eight years as galley slaves (prisoners chained to, and forced to pull, the oars of an oared fighting ship, or galley).

Sir Francis Drake attacks a Spanish treasure ship.

Humiliated by an unsuccessful voyage and a ringing defeat, Hawkins later accused Drake of deserting him. "The Judith," he said, "forsooke us in our great myserie." It was the only time in Drake's extraordinary career that anyone ever accused him of cowardice. The two men eventually reconciled, but it took years to heal their mutual wounds.

Drake never forgot the Spanish viceroy's treachery. Historian Peter Pierson called it "the defining moment" of Drake's life. After the defeat, he devoted himself to piracy and war—his own private war—against Spain.

THREE
Plundering the Spanish Main

The Spanish treachery at San Juan de Ulúa marked the end of English attempts to trade with the Spaniards in the New World during the sixteenth century. It also signaled the start of a relentless campaign against the Spanish by Elizabethan sea dogs. After Ulúa, Francis Drake became famous, heading the list of the queen's most notable mariners. Other seasoned English seamen included John Hawkins, Martin Frobisher, and John Lovell, among many others. But none harbored a greater hatred for the Spaniards than Drake.

Drake hated the Spaniards not only for their treachery in New Spain, but also because of their faith. He viewed the Roman Catholic Church as anti-Christian and Philip II of Spain as its chief advocate. Philip in fact believed that his mission in life was to gain world dominance for Spain and the Church of Rome. Drake opposed Philip and all he represented. After marrying Mary Newman in 1569, Drake

Martin Frobisher, another great English mariner of Drake's day

began his private war against the Spanish monarch—that is, he became a pirate.

In 1570, Drake left his bride of a few months and returned to the Caribbean on a scouting mission. He intended, according to a biographical account of the voyage written in 1592 and published in 1626, "to gaine such intelligences as might further him to get some amends for his losse [at San Juan de Ulúa]." Drake scoured the Caribbean that year, and again in 1571, searching for weaknesses in Spain's overstretched colonial defenses, which ringed the Caribbean Sea from Florida to the mouth of the Orinoco River. Little is known of

Philip II ruled Spain at the height of its power.

his first cruise in 1570, but his next voyage in 1571 was successful and profitable.

Captaining the twenty-five-ton *Swan*, Drake explored the waters off the Isthmus of Panama. He wanted to investigate the possibility of attacking Nombre de Dios, the collection point for all the Peruvian treasure and the destination of the second of the two annual flotas from Spain. Off the coast of Darien he found a tiny natural harbor, screened from view by thick vegetation. Fish were abundant in the shielded waters, as were fresh fruit and pheasants in the surrounding jungle. Drake named his sanctuary Port Pheasant.

This map, from a sixteenth century atlas, shows part of Spain's vast holdings in the New World.

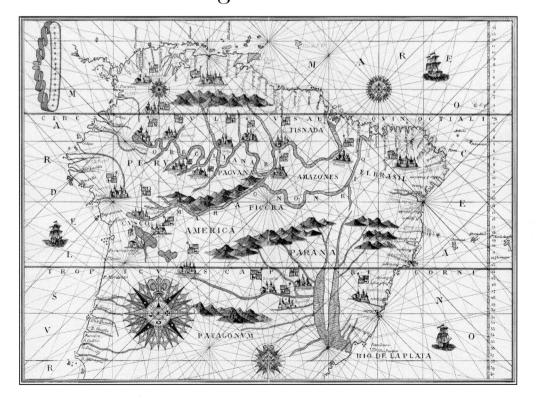

THE CIMMARONES

The Cimmarones (sometimes called Cimaroons) were escaped African slaves who resisted Spanish authority. Their name derives from *cimarrón*, Spanish for "wild, unruly, or untamed." Over time, they intermarried with the local natives and formed two new tribes. They lived off the land, in hiding in the Central American jungles, and waged an ongoing guerilla war against their former Spanish masters.

Their hatred of the Spaniards drove the Cimarrones to harass Spanish colonists, burn their farms, rob them of their gold and other valuables, and often kill them. Gold meant little to the Cimarrones. It was too soft for making weapons. They used iron for weapons and gold only for making ornaments. But they enjoyed stealing Spanish gold, simply because they knew how much the Spaniards worshiped it. They befriended Francis Drake—a fellow enemy of the Spaniards—and guided him to Spanish treasure several times.

Operating from this tiny base in the middle of enemy country, Drake and about thirty bold men preyed on Spanish shipping with great success, capturing two frigates (three-masted square-rigged ships with twenty-four to thirty-eight guns on a single deck) and about twenty smaller vessels. Drake cautioned the captain and crew of at least one Spanish frigate—and likely many others—that the English "are well disposed if there be no cause to the contrary; if there be cause, we will be devils rather than men." Despite the threatening tone of his words, however, Drake rarely harmed an enemy.

Beyond his activities on the high seas, Drake conducted daring raids into the Panamanian interior, some in concert with Cimarrones, escaped African slaves and their offspring. No longer a slave trader, Drake had befriended them to further his own treasure-seeking interests. But as he came to know them, Drake began to see the former slaves not as "merchandise"—as he once had—but as human beings. He grew to respect and admire them.

In return, the Cimarrones bonded with the Englishmen. They willingly joined the fight against the hated Spaniards who had once enslaved them, often carrying the packs of Drake's men, who wilted in the tropical heat. If an Englishman collapsed, "two [cimarrones] would carry him with ease between them," passing him to two others every two miles or so, until the seaman recovered.

Drake developed a lightning-quick style of attack that featured a headlong strike to unsettle his enemy, followed by rapid deployment—tactics that he would later use at sea. He and his crew attacked gold- and silver-bearing mule trains on jungle trails and treasure-laden barges on the Chagres River—all bound for Nombre de Dios—with equal abandon and success.

A sixteenth-century Spanish document notes:

Upon the coast of Nombre de Diós [Drake] *did rob diverse barques* [three-masted ships with both square- and fore-and-aft-rigged sails] *in the river of Chagres, and in the same river did rob diverse barques that were transporting of merchandise of forty thousand ducats* [gold coins of varying value] *and velvets and taffetas, besides other merchandise with gold and silver in other barques, and with the same came to Plymouth, where it was divided amongst his partners.*

Drake was rapidly becoming a wealthy man—the hard way.

On one occasion, Drake disguised himself as a Spanish merchant and visited Nombre de Dios to better familiarize himself with the treasure port. He found the town that he aptly called "the treasure house of the world" to be poorly defended. Before leaving the Spanish Main for Plymouth in the late summer of 1571, Drake buried a cache of supplies ashore at Port Pheasant. Nombre de Dios could clearly expect to receive a second visit from Elizabeth's foremost sea dog.

Drake returned to the Panamanian coast in June 1572, now as captain of John Hawkins's forty-ton *Pascoe*. The *Swan*, captained by Drake's brother John, accompanied him, along with seventy-three crewmen. Joseph, another of Drake's three brothers, was among them. Landing at Port Pheasant on July 12, Drake found a message left by his "verie loving friend, John Garret," who had sailed with him the year before and had stayed in the Caribbean with a small trading vessel. Garret's message warned, "Captain Drake, if you fortune to come into this port make haste away; for the Spaniards, which you had with you last year [Spanish prisoners whom Drake had released] have betrayed this place, and taken away all that is left here."

Not one to pass up a challenge, Drake instead set his men to constructing a log stockade, while he completed plans to raid Nombre de Dios. At that point, James Raunse, who had served as mate aboard the *William and John* during John Hawkins's final slave-trading voyage, put into Port Pheasant with thirty men. Raunse agreed to toss in his lot with Drake.

On the night of July 28–29, Drake and a boat of pirates left Port Pheasant and slipped into the harbor of Nombre de Dios and attempted to sack the town. But Drake's plans went drastically wrong. At three o'clock in the morning, the town militia discovered his raiders and a violent struggle began in the town square. Drake and his men drove off the militiamen, but he and several of his raiders were wounded and withdrew to their ships. The raid failed miserably. Raunse decided to give up and left Drake to set up another base of operations ashore in the Gulf of San Blas. But Drake was not yet finished with Nombre de Dios.

While awaiting the arrival of another flota, Drake cruised the Spanish Main as far east as Curaçao looking for prizes. In January 1573, he received word that the Spanish flota would return to Nombre de Dios in April. Drake returned to the Panamanian jungle to lay the groundwork for another attack. Once the flota arrived, gold and other valuables were sent through the jungle from Panama by mule train for shipment to Spain. Drake figured that it would be easier to seize the Spanish treasure before it reached Nombre de Dios than to wait until it was loaded aboard the ships.

On February 11, 1573, while patrolling with a group of Cimarrones, Drake reached the top of a high ridge about halfway across the Isthmus of Panama. The Cimarrones showed him a lone tree with handgrips carved into its side and encouraged Drake to climb it for a better view. To the east he could see the Atlantic Ocean. And to the west lay a broad expanse of green water, shimmering in the sunlight and stretching all the way to the horizon—the Pacific Ocean! It was the first time an Englishman had looked upon Magellan's magnificent Mar Pacifico. Back on the ground, Drake, overcome with emotion, knelt and prayed, imploring "Almighty God of His Goodness to give him life and leave to sail once in an English ship on that sea." Visions of what lay beyond that distant horizon already danced in his mind. But first, there was work to be done.

Early in April, he met a French pirate ship commanded by Guillaume Le Testu. The two captains agreed to join forces and split whatever profit might result from a joint venture against the flota. About a week later, a force of English, French, and Cimarrón raiders attacked a treasure-bearing mule train about a mile from Nombre de Dios. They chased away the guards, buried the silver, and fled with as much gold

Treasure—including gold, silver, porcelain, and an astrolabe (an early navigational instrument)—recovered from a Spanish galleon that sank off the coast of Cuba in 1590

as they could carry. Le Testu was wounded during the assault and left to die on the road. The Spaniards later recovered much of their silver, but most of the raiders returned to their ships safely to split their gold equally. Drake paid a dear price, however. He lost two of his brothers on the expedition, John to a Spanish bullet, Joseph to disease. And he was forced to abandon the *Swan*.

Drake and his crew sailed for home in August 1573 with a share totaling about twenty thousand pounds—a tremendous sum in those days. His next voyage would elevate him to a higher plane—and ensure his place in history.

Sir Francis Drake's Route

← First Voyage 1567
← Second Voyage 1569
← Third Voyage 1577–1580

FOUR

Circling the Globe

When Drake returned home with his stolen treasure in 1573, he found that diplomatic relations, if not trust, between England and Spain were improving. Queen Elizabeth and her advisers worried that Drake's latest exploits in the Caribbean might anger King Philip II of Spain. Drake decided to suspend, temporarily, any further actions against Spain.

In 1575, now a wealthy shipowner, Drake committed himself and his ships to England's effort to subdue Ireland. The Irish had been up in arms since 1494 when England's Henry VII attempted to subordinate Ireland's parliament (lawmaking body). Irish anger turned to fury after 1541 when Henry VIII tried to impose on Ireland his religious changes—that is, his conversion from Catholicism to Protestantism. Drake commanded a small naval force and paid the entire cost of the fleet. One of Drake's contemporaries wrote:

The Latin inscription on this engraving translates as "Francis Drake, Noble English Knight."

He furnished at his own propper charge, three friggots [frigates] with men, munition, and served voluntary in Ireland under Walter [Devereaux, earl] of Essex: where he did excellent service, both by Sea, and land, at the winning of divers strong Forts.

Drake learned more of military operations, while cultivating the friendship of Essex and soldiers such as Captain Thomas Doughty. The campaign in Ireland also gave Drake another outlet for his lifelong hatred of Catholicism.

From 1576 to 1578, tensions between England and Spain rose again over the Netherlands, where Protestants were rebelling against Spanish rule. Drake saw this as an appropriate time to renew his private war against the Spaniards, and perhaps even to carry it into the Pacific. With the help of his new friends—Essex, Thomas Doughty, and others— Drake won the queen's support for a voyage to the Pacific.

Elizabeth, although wary of Spain's strength, saw an opportunity to take advantage of its weaknesses—namely, the undefended treasure ports on the Pacific side of Central and South America. According to Drake, the queen said to him, "I would gladly be revenged on the King of Spain for divers injuries that I have received, and you are the only man that might do this exploit." Private investors backed the expedition, with the queen personally contributing 1,000 crowns (about £250).

Drake sailed from Plymouth on a wintry day in mid-December 1577, aboard the 150-ton, 18-gun *Pelican* (which he later renamed *Golden Hind*). Four other vessels accompanied him: the 80-ton, 11-gun *Elizabeth*, the 30-ton, 6-gun *Marigold*, the 50-ton, 5-gun flyboat or provision ship *Swan* (not the same *Swan* abandoned in the Caribbean), and the 17-ton pinnace *Benedict*, a small ship used a tender, or a small vessel used to attend (as to supply provisions) a warship, and armed only with small-caliber guns.

The GOLDEN HIND, Drake's tiny flagship, sails through the windswept Straits of Magellan.

The ships carried a complement of about 170 men, although Drake's cousin John Drake said in 1587, "Between men of war and mariners, the whole armada included a hundred and forty men." His count likely excluded a number of ship's boys and some fifteen gentleman adventurers along for pleasure and profit. Notable were two of Drake's closest friends, Thomas and John Doughty. From his own family, Drake also took his youngest brother, Thomas.

Officially, the queen's instructions for the voyage told Drake to sail through the Strait of Magellan, search out potential sites for English colonies in the undeveloped southern regions of South America, and

Life at Sea

Discipline, hard work, hardship, and danger filled the life of a sixteenth-century sailor. A ship's captain was master of everything aboard his ship. At sea, his rule was law. He held the power of life and death and punished criminal offenders severely. A thief would have his head shaved and smeared with hot tar. For threatening an officer with a knife, a seaman would have his right hand chopped off. And a murderer would find himself bound to his victim, face-to-face, and tossed overboard.

The master, or navigating officer, and the quartermaster reported directly to the captain. Respectively, they navigated and steered the ship. Tradesmen kept the ship in good repair and working order. A boatswain (the word is pronounced bo'-sun) had charge of sails, anchors, and rigging, while a chief gunner looked after the ship's weapons, particularly the cannons. A sailmaker patched and mended sails, a caulker kept the ship watertight, a cooper cared for the barrels containing water and supplies, and swabbers continually scrubbed the ship's oak

return home the way he had come. Unofficially, Drake was to raid the Peruvian ports from which the Spanish treasure ships sailed. This part of the mission was not committed to writing, of course, as England and Spain were not at war. Consequently, Elizabeth could not grant Drake a privateer's license, which allowed private vessels to take "prizes" in

decks with seawater to keep them from drying out and springing leaks. Work hours were long, and the work was hard.

The captain and his officers slept in bunks in private cabins, whereas the common seaman had no place of his own and slept wherever he could find a spot, below deck in cold weather or topside in mild weather. A typical diet at sea consisted of biscuit, cheese, and meat and fish that were preserved in barrels of salt. Sailors often developed scurvy—a disease brought on by a lack of vitamin C and causing lethargy, loss of teeth, and pains in the limbs.

At many exotic ports, mariners risked the dangers of contracting life-threatening diseases—dysentery, typhus fever, cholera, and more—and confronting hostile natives. At sea, they faced constant danger from shipboard fires, violent storms, and pirates. For those who went to sea, life was anything but easy.

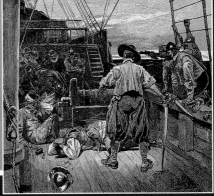

A nineteenth-century American magazine illustration shows Drake's crew seizing a Spanish treasure ship off the coast of Chile.

time of war. In short, Drake's unofficial mission called for acts of piracy. But if Drake was caught, the queen would not protect him. He was on his own.

Drake sailed down the African coast to the Cape Verde Islands, capturing a Portuguese ship, the *Santa Maria*, along the way. He kept the vessel's captain, Nuña da Silva, aboard the *Pelican*. Da Silva was a seasoned navigator and familiar with the route to South America. Drake, who had sailed without charts of the Pacific, planned to exploit Da Silva's navigational skills. He restocked the *Santa Maria* with his own men, renamed it *Mary* after his wife, and set the rest of the Portuguese sailors adrift in a pinnace. Drake put Thomas Doughty in command of the *Mary*, which ultimately proved to be a big mistake.

Leaving the Cape Verde Islands behind, Drake roughly followed Ferdinand Magellan's route across the Atlantic and down the east coast of South America. Magellan, a Portuguese navigator working for Spain, had crossed the Pacific, only to die in a battle with natives on Mactan Island in the Philippines in 1521. But 17 of the 237 seamen who had begun the voyage—later captained by Juan Sebastián de Elcano—completed the first circumnavigation of the globe in 1522.

During the Atlantic crossing, Drake learned that Thomas Doughty had revealed the real purpose of Drake's voyage to Lord Burleigh, the lord treasurer of England, before the fleet sailed. Burleigh feared the disastrous effect a pirating voyage might have on English relations with Spain, which had already been strained by Drake's earlier voyages. Burleigh tried and failed to stop the voyage but apparently persuaded Doughty to disrupt the voyage in any way possible.

After a stormy passage, the fleet arrived in Port Saint Julian, just north of the Strait of Magellan, on June 20, 1578. Drake immediately charged Thomas Doughty with mutiny and tried him, near the remnants of a gallows where Magellan had quelled a mutiny some fifty-eight years earlier. Francis Pretty, one of Drake's gentlemen at arms, later described the proceedings, in part, this way:

> *In this port our General* [Drake] *began to enquire diligently of the actions of Master Thomas Doughty, and found them not to be such as he looked for, but tending rather of contention or mutiny, or some*

other disorder, whereby, without redress, the success of the voyage might greatly have been hazarded. Whereupon the company was called together and made acquainted with the particulars of the cause, which were found, partly by Master Doughty's own confession, and partly by the evidence of the fact, to be true. . . . So that the cause being thoroughly heard, and all things done in good order as near as might be to the course of our laws in England, it was concluded that Master Doughty should receive punishment according to the quality of the offence. [Doughty then requested and took communion with Drake and the company's chaplain]. *Which being done, and the place of execution made ready, he* [Doughty] *having embraced our General, and taken his leave of all the company, with prayers for the Queen's Majesty and our realm, in quiet sort laid his head to the block, where he ended his life.*

Drake held up the severed head before his assembled crew and said, "This is the end of traitors." The stocky sea captain could act ruthlessly when he deemed it necessary. Doughty's death ended all talk of mutiny on the expedition.

Drake spent the next two months in Port Saint Julian, repairing his ships and reducing his flotilla to the best three vessels, then sailed on to the Strait of Magellan. The strait is a winding, 350-mile-long passage, lined with glacier-ridden, cloud-shrouded mountains and swept by icy winds. It separates the southern tip of South America from the large island of Tierra del Fuego. They reached it on August 21, 1578. Before entering, Drake paused to rename his flagship *Golden Hind*, in honor of one of his backers whose coat of arms bore a golden deer.

A half-century earlier, it had taken Magellan thirty-eight days to navigate the treacherous channel. Drake did it in sixteen days. But when he entered the Pacific, a violent storm struck, scattering his three ships. The *Marigold* sank, and all its hands were lost. The *Elizabeth* sailed back through the strait for home. Drake found his fleet reduced to a

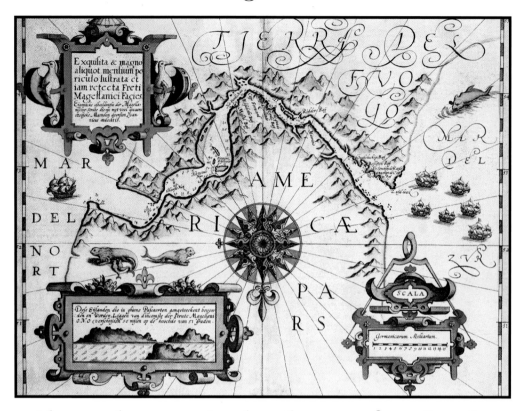

This map, drawn circa 1600, shows the Straits of Magellan—the treacherous passage at the southernmost tip of South America.

single vessel. Francis Fletcher, the Hind's chaplain, described the mood of the mariners:

> God seemed to set Himself against us . . . as if he had pronounced a sentence not to stay His hand . . . till He had buried our bodies and ships also, in the bottomless depth of the raging sea.

The storm drove the *Golden Hind* 600 miles (966 kilometers) to the south before the skies cleared 53 days later. Drake discovered that Tierra del Fuego was an island and not a continent to the south then known as *Terra Australis Incognita*—Latin for "unknown southern land." His finding revealed another way around South America, via the waters south of Cape Horn. Today's navigators know the route as Drake Passage, where, as Francis Fletcher put it, two oceans become "one and the self same sea."

Drake turned the *Golden Hind* northward and made sail for Valparaíso, Chile. He stopped once along the coast and encountered hostile natives. The natives killed four of his men, wounded six more, and struck Drake under his right eye with an arrow. Drake enjoyed better luck in Valparaíso. Arriving on December 5, he relieved a Spanish merchant ship of its cargo of gold, wine, and food without firing a shot. Continuing up the coast, he raided the undefended ports of Arica and Callao, Peru, while taking more prizes at sea.

At Callao, Drake learned of a great prize, a ship named the *Nuestra Señora de la Concepción*, making for Panama with a huge load of silver. (Spanish mariners nicknamed the ship *Cacafuego*, or "Spitfire," because it was one of the few ships in the "peaceful" waters of the Pacific to carry cannon.) Ignoring rumors of two Spanish warships searching for him, Drake gave chase and caught up with the *Cacafuego* on March 1, 1579. The *Golden Hind*'s cannon blasted the Spaniard's mizzenmast apart, and the English ship drew alongside the crippled Spanish vessel. Drake's men boarded the *Cacafuego* and quickly overcame its crew.

The Englishmen needed four more days to transfer the *Cacafuego*'s magnificent cargo to the *Golden Hind*—thirteen chests of silver coin, twenty-six tons of silver bars, eighty pounds of gold, and lockers of pearls and precious gems. The haul assured the success of Drake's expedition. Drake now began to think about how best to get home with his loot. To return the way he had come posed the threat of encountering a host of angry Spaniards. He opted to seek an alternate route: a western approach to the long-sought Northwest Passage—a sea passage between the Atlantic and Pacific Oceans around the North American land barrier. (This sea route was not successfully navigated until 1906.)

Pirates board a merchant ship.

Drake cruised north in the summer of 1579, plundering off the coast of Central America and New Spain along the way, but failed to find the Northwest Passage. Extreme cold halted him somewhere south of Vancouver Island, and he turned south again. He had captured a chart of the Pacific from a prize taken off Central America. If Magellan could cross the Pacific safely, Drake decided, so could he!

In preparation for the crossing, Drake repaired the *Golden Hind* in a sheltered bay on the foggy coast of northern California. The inlet where he is thought to have landed is now called Drake's Bay (although the exact location of the bay remains hotly contested to this day). Frank Pretty, one of Drake's "gentlemen at arms," wrote:

[Drake] *called this country Nova Albion* [Nova, Latin for "new"; Albion, is the Roman name for England], *and that for two causes; the one in respect of the white banks and cliffs* [reminiscent of the

44

chalk cliffs of Dover], *which lie towards the sea, and the other, because it might have some affinity with our country in name, which sometime was so called.*

Drake left a plate claiming "her Majesty's right and title" to the land "wherein there is not some probable show of gold or silver."

The *Golden Hind* sailed west in July 1579. Crossing 7,000 miles of Pacific in 68 days, the *Hind* touched first at Palau in the Caroline Islands, then at Mindanao, in what Spain had recently named the

A map, drawn in Antwerp in 1570, showing the islands of the West Indies

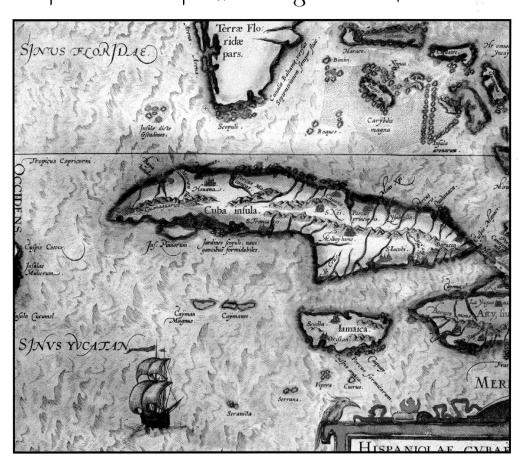

Philippines in honor of King Philip II. In the fabled Spice Islands (the Moluccas), Drake added six tons of cloves to his valuable cargo, along with generous quantities of bananas, ginger, peppers, rice, and sugarcane.

As it continued on to the Celebes, Drake's extraordinary voyage almost ended tragically, when, according to his own account, the low-riding *Hind* "laid up fast upon a desperate shoal." But as luck often favors the bold, a shift in the wind and high tide floated the little ship, miraculously without severe hull damage.

After stops at the islands of Timor and Java, (both in present-day Indonesia), Drake set course for home, still some ten thousand miles distant. Little is known of his voyage across the Indian Ocean, around the Cape of Good Hope, up the west African coast, past Spain and Britanny, and at long last to England. After an absence of almost three years, the *Golden Hind* sailed into Plymouth on September 26, 1580. As the *Hind* entered port, Drake likely breathed a silent prayer for the queen's good health—for Elizabeth was the only person who could shield him against Spanish charges of piracy.

F I V E

El Draque Returns

When Drake first approached Plymouth harbor—the first English captain and only the second ship's master to sail around the globe—he hailed two men in a fishing boat. "Be the queen alive and well?" he reportedly shouted. They answered, yes, doubtlessly triggering a sigh of relief in the barrel-chested navigator.

Drake's booty, estimated at a half-million pounds in Elizabethan currency, was offloaded at Plymouth and hauled overland to the Tower of London, while Drake sailed the *Golden Hind* over to Deptford. His share of the profits totaled at least ten thousand pounds. Today, the entire treasure would be worth more than £68 million, with Drake's share totaling about £1.36 million (or about $42 million and $840,000 respectively). Drake immediately invested in an estate near Plymouth, Buckland Abbey, and lavished gifts on the queen's courtiers. Elizabeth in turn gave him other estates and

Queen Elizabeth I knights Drake on board the GOLDEN HIND.

knighted him in 1581, dubbing him "the master thief of the unknown world."

Drake soon learned that relations between Elizabeth I and Philip II had not improved in his absence. Philip, in fact, had taken control of Portugal in 1580 and acquired a large armada, which he was refitting to escort flotas to the Caribbean. Philip had keenly felt the impact of El Draque's piracies in the New World. And Spain's ambassador was complaining to Elizabeth about "the plunders committed by this vile corsair [pirate]." Drake laid low for the next five years.

The now-legendary sea dog temporarily retired to Buckland Abbey. His ship was laid up in dry dock as a memorial to Drake and his voyage

Elizabeth Sydenham, Sir Francis Drake's second wife

CARTAGENA

Francis Drake's fleet, diminished and weakened by disease, arrived outside Cartagena on February 9, 1586. Forewarned of El Draque's earlier assault upon Santo Domingo, Pedro Fernández de Bustos, the port city's governor, had prepared for the dreaded Englishman's arrival. He had assembled a defense force comprising 54 horsemen, 450 harquebusiers (foot soldiers armed with matchlock guns fired from a hooked gun rest), 100 spearmen, 20 armed black slaves, and 400 Indian archers. Moreover, veteran Spanish commander Pedro Vique Manrique stood offshore with two galleys (low seagoing vessels propelled by oars) bristling with guns. To Drake's advantage, however, rumors of the unparalleled size of his fleet had demoralized the defenders before a shot was fired.

Drake attacked straight through Cartagena's vast outer harbor at two the next morning, landing 600 men under

around the world. In semi-retirement, Drake served twice as mayor of Plymouth and in Parliament. Tragedy touched him in 1583 when his wife died. Two years later, he remarried, this time wedding Elizabeth Sydenham, the beautiful daughter of one of England's wealthiest families. As with his first wife, he went to sea again shortly after the wedding.

In 1584, William I, prince of Orange was shot and killed by a Catholic fanatic. William I had been the driving force behind the Dutch

Christopher Carleill. Meanwhile, Martin Frobisher, another of Elizabeth's famed sea dogs, led a tiny fleet of pinnaces against the fortress at Boquerón. At first light, Carleill's column smashed through a shaky defense line and sent fearful shock waves rippling throughout the ranks of Bustos's remaining defenders. The corsairs ran Vique's galleys aground. Their panic-stricken crews abandoned them, splashing their way ashore through the surf, hotly pursued by revolting galley slaves. Bustos surrendered Cartagena after only two days of fighting—a testament to Drake's generalship.

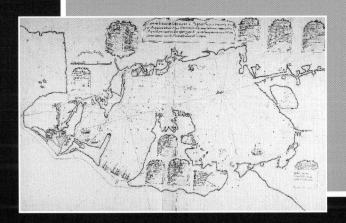

The South American seaport of Cartagena, as shown in an eighteenth-century Spanish map

revolt against Spanish rule in the Netherlands. The Dutch appealed to Elizabeth for help, as Spanish forces marched relentlessly across the southern Netherlands and closed in on Antwerp. She sent a small force to the Netherlands. Philip responded by ordering the arrest of all English ships in Spanish ports in retaliation for piracies "beyond the line." When Elizabeth recognized that she could no longer avoid the long-anticipated war with Spain, she once again summoned her favorite sea dog.

El Draque Returns

On September 14, 1585, Sir Francis Drake went to sea, in command of a fleet of some two dozen ships and eight pinnaces carrying over two thousand seamen and soldiers. The queen played her usual double game. Publicly, Elizabeth commissioned Drake to rescue English prisoners held in Spanish mainland ports. But privately, she authorized his "descent of the Indies" for still another campaign of plunder and profit. Private investors—including the queen—again financed the voyage. They expected a fat return on their investment. Elizabeth also hoped that England's first act of open war with Spain would weaken Spain's finances and prestige in Europe.

Drake and his pirates carried out the first part of their assignment with threatening visits to Bayonna and Vigo on the Spanish coast. After finding that the arrests had been lifted and that no English subjects needed rescuing, they took booty and sailed on. At the Cape Verde Islands, they seized the town of Santiago and held it for ransom. When none was paid, Drake's men burned Santiago to the ground and sailed for the Indies.

The pirates reached Santo Domingo (in the present-day Dominican Republic) on New Year's Eve of 1585, and captured the city without a struggle the next day. The Spaniards refused Drake's demands for a million ducats in ransom. After burning about a third of the city to the ground, he settled for 25,000 ducats. He later wrote:

> And albeit for divers days together we ordeined each morning by daybreake, until the heat began at nine of the clocke, that 200 Mariners did nought else but labour to fire and burne the said houses . . . yet did wee not . . . And so in the end, what wearied with firing, and what hastened by some other respects, we were contented to accept five and twentie thousand ducats.

As additional ransom, they also took all the gold, silver, and jewels that they could lay their hands on—even the bells from the churches.

Shortly after its arrival in Santo Domingo, a contagious fever struck the fleet, wiping out hundreds and leaving the survivors muddled and weak. They stayed a month, then sailed south for Cartagena, arriving on February 9. They quickly subdued the city and again demanded ransom, this time about a half-million ducats. But Drake's men found the plunder pitifully small. Word had reached Cartagena a month before the English arrived that El Draque was on the prowl again and breathing fire. The city's residents had hidden their valuables inland.

As his men continued to die from a new disease—probably malaria—Drake abandoned his plan to use Cartagena as a base of operations for another raid on Nombre de Dios and Panama. Instead, he finally accepted 110,000 ducats and the city's guns in ransom and set sail for home. Along the way, Drake's corsairs destroyed Saint Augustine, Spain's colony in Florida, and picked up the survivors of the failed English colony on Roanoke Island.

Drake's decimated fleet arrived home on July 28, 1586, carrying booty estimated at £60,000 (today about $503,704 U.S.). The surviving crew members—about 750 men had died, most of disease—divided about a third of that amount. Drake's backers received only about a 75 percent return on their investment. Drake himself also lost money. Financially, the expedition had ended in failure. Politically, however, El Draque's return to the Caribbean had rocked the very foundations of the Spanish Empire. But from the Dragon's perspective, the best was still to come.

SIX

Philip's Grand Armada

Although Drake's latest assault on Spain's New World empire proved unsuccessful for his backers, it bordered on total disaster for King Philip. His colonial defenses were undermined, his commerce was shattered, and critical Spanish credit in the great banks of Europe was severely damaged. He could not allow this stunning blow to Spain's dwindling prestige to pass unpunished. It was time, he concluded, to carry the war to England and "put fire into their house." Philip decided to move forward quickly with what he called the "Enterprise of England"—his plan to invade England. To this end, he was already gathering the greatest fleet ever before assembled—the Spanish Armada.

Elizabeth was aware of Philip's intentions and progress. In March 1587, she called once again on Sir Francis Drake to attack the ships assembling for Philip's Spanish Armada. Although the queen hoped to slow Philip's advance, piracy remained her prime motivation. A joint-

The Spanish Armada, sent by Philip II to attack England

---

stock company financed the voyage, and Drake set to sea out of Plymouth on April 2, 1587, with a fleet of 23 ships and about 2,100 men.

Drake knew that the main port of assembly for the Armada was Lisbon, but access to its harbor along the long, narrow, and heavily defended Tagus River was difficult. Instead, he attacked the more exposed Bay of Cádiz, which he took completely by surprise. Drake's privateers, now legally authorized by the queen to seek revenge against Spain, destroyed or captured some thirty-six ships and tons of supplies intended to join the Armada.

Doubling back to Lisbon, Drake missed intercepting a returning flota by two days. Drake's fleet next cruised off Cape Saint Vincent, where they found good hunting. Drake later reported that between April 27 and May 26,

> *It hath pleased God that we have taken forts, ships, barks, carvels* [small vessels with triangular sails], *and divers other vessels more than a hundred, most laden, some with oars for galleys, planks and timber for ships and pinnaces, hoops and pipe-staves for cask* [barrels], *with many other provisions for this great army.*

Drake rightly figured that the loss of hoops and staves—the basic parts needed to make barrels—was most critical to Spain's cause, for the Armada could not sail against England without barrels of water and supplies.

The privateers next headed for the Azores in search of further prizes. On June 9, Drake's fleet surrounded a Spanish ship and forced its surrender. The vessel turned out to be the *San Felipe*—the king of Spain's own galleon—returning from the East Indies with a cargo valued at £114,000. (Today, the cargo's value would total about £15.5 million or $9.6 million.) The privateers then turned for home with the richest prize ever taken at the time.

Drake's successful expedition would delay the sailing date of Philip's Grand Armada by about a year. Upon his arrival in Plymouth, on June 26, Drake told his supporters that "he had singed the King of Spain's beard." But in a letter to Sir Francis Walsingham, England's secretary of state, Drake cautioned, "Prepare in England strongly, and most by sea. Stop him [Philip] now, and stop him ever!"

The Armada finally sailed from Lisbon on May 20, 1588, captained by Don Alonzo Perez de Guzman, duke of Medina Sidonia, an inexperienced warrior. His fleet now numbered 130 ships, some 8,000 seamen, and perhaps as many as 19,000 soldiers. To challenge the Spanish threat, Elizabeth had assembled a fleet of 34 of her own ships and about 163 mostly small privateering vessels. (In actual tonnage, the

English fleet weighed about the same as the Armada.) The queen handed command of her fleet to Charles Howard, second Baron Howard of Effingham, and appointed Sir Francis Drake vice admiral and second in command. Lord Howard divided his fleet into four squadrons, with himself, Drake, John Hawkins, and Martin Frobisher each commanding a group.

Storms delayed the Armada's arrival off England's shores for more than two months. The English first sighted it off Cornwall's Lizard Point on July 29, 1588. Legend has it that Howard and Drake were engaged in a game of bowles (similar to the Italian bocce ball) on the Plymouth Hoe when news of the Armada reached them. Drake reputedly

---

According to a famous story, the Armada was approaching—but Drake calmly continued with his game of bowls.

exhorted his companion to keep on playing, calmly suggesting, "There is plenty of time to finish the game and beat the Spaniards, too." Whether or not these words accurately reflect Drake's reaction to the Armada's arrival, they sound in character and make for a good tale. In any case, the larger part of Lord Howard's fleet began clearing Plymouth harbor that night.

The Spanish usually employed ships as floating fortresses and carried garrisons of land soldiers to board enemy vessels. The English, on the other hand, emphasized fast ships, nimble seamanship, and expert gunnery at a longer range—practices developed by Drake and other innovative sea dogs on the Spanish Main and elsewhere. Also, English sailors trained in boarding ships and hand-to-hand fighting techniques eliminated the need for a ship to carry a garrison of soldiers. These contrasting tactics clashed in three encounters: off Plymouth, July 31; off Portland Bill, August 2; and off the Isle of Wight, August 4.

Medina Sidonia's orders called for him to sail up the English Channel to the Netherlands and pick up more invasion troops from the Spanish army operating there. Howard's mission was to break up the Armada before it reached the Netherlands.

The English fleet maneuvered to the windward side and rear of the Spaniards, enabling Lord Howard's ships to move swiftly with a following wind. Medina Sidonia, in response, formed his fleet into a near-impenetrable crescent-shaped formation that he sustained almost all the way up the Channel. Harassing the Spaniards at long range, the Englishmen avoided enemy attempts to draw them into close action but failed to inflict any serious damage on the Armada.

On Sunday, August 31, 1588, Vice Admiral Sir Francis Drake, in his flagship *Revenge*, engaged the Grand Armada off Plymouth. He paired off with his counterpart, the Spanish vice admiral *(almirante*

Fire Ships

Fire ships played an important role in sixteenth-century warfare at sea. A fire ship was usually a small vessel of little value. It was loaded with combustibles and explosives and fitted with special ventilating ducts to ensure rapid combustion. A slow match and a train of gunpowder were used to ignite the explosive charge.

In battle, or when attacking enemy ships at anchor, the fire ships sailed as close to an intended victim as possible. Its crew often lashed the steering wheel to keep the ship on course until it drew close enough to secure it to the victim with grappling irons. A seaman would then ignite the slow match. The captain and crew would escape in a boat towed astern (behind) or alongside.

The English launch fire ships against the Spanish Armada.

general) Juan Martinez de Recalde. As the battle progressed, the larger Spanish vessels closed to support Recalde. Rather than risk a boarding action, the English broke the engagement. The Armada closed ranks and continued its ponderous march up the English Channel.

During the first night of a weeklong chase, Fleet Commander Lord Howard designated Drake to lead the English fleet up the Channel by the light of his stern lantern. In regrouping, however, the *Nuestra Señora del Rosario*, flagship of one of the Spanish squadrons, was damaged in a collision with another ship. Drake sighted the *Rosario*, doused his stern light, left station, and captured the crippled vessel. Meanwhile,

---

A portrait of Sir Francis Drake

Sir Martin Frobisher, Drake's great rival

Howard unknowingly followed a Spanish lantern through the night and almost joined ranks with the Armada.

Drake later claimed that he had sighted ships working upwind during the night. Thinking them to be Spanish, he had given chase. The ships had turned out to be German, but then Drake had sighted the *Rosario*. Howard accepted Drake's defense, mildly rebuking him for leaving station. But rival sea dog Martin Frobisher felt less charitable. He challenged Drake's actions and rights to the spoils and threatened "to make him spend the best blood in his belly." Frobisher never made good on his threat.

On August 6, Medina Sidonia, hoping to load troops from Flanders, ordered his fleet to anchor in an exposed position off Calais. The next day, Drake, in the four-hundred-ton *Revenge*, merged his squadron with Howard's, also off Calais, west of the Armada. At midnight on August 7, Drake, Hawkins, and others sent fire ships into the midst of the anchored Spanish fleet. Amid cries of "the devil ships are coming," the Spaniards panicked, cut their anchor chains, and fled. Gusty prevailing winds drove them swiftly toward the North Sea.

Drake and his squadron led the English attack in the climactic eight-hour battle that ensued off Gravelines, a port in northern France, sinking several Spanish ships and driving the others into the North Sea. The English ships returned to port for supplies on August 12, their ammunition gone. The Spanish ships, unable to double back against the wind, sailed around the north of Scotland and west of Ireland to return home. They wrecked twenty-eight ships on their return voyage. In the end, fewer than half of the ships and only one of every three men in Philip's Grand Armada made it back to Spain. English losses numbered about sixty men, but not a single ship. After reading a report on his Armada's defeat, Philip remarked, "I have read it all, although I would rather not have done, because it hurts so much."

A design for a tapestry showing the defeat of
the Spanish Armada

In defeating the Armada, England claimed Spain's prestige and power for itself and laid the cornerstone of the British Empire. Vice Admiral Sir Francis Drake, already his nation's most famous hero and greatest sea dog, received perhaps more than his fair share of credit for England's huge triumph. But that is often the case in the lives of national heroes. In the seven-plus years left to him, Drake would earn no further glory.

Afterword

After the Spanish Armada's defeat, Sir Francis Drake received one more order from the queen. The remnants of the Armada had fled to the north coast of Spain. Elizabeth wanted them destroyed. In 1589, she appointed Drake to command a naval force of about 150 royal and private vessels and Sir John Norris to lead a landing force of roughly 19,000 troops. The force landed at La Caruña and Lisbon, Portugal. They achieved little and soon returned to England, disappointed and riddled by disease.

Five years later, the queen once more called on her favorite sea dog. It would be the last call for "a daring navigator and prince of corsairs," as nineteenth-century biographer Sir Julian S. Corbett called Drake. In 1595, the queen ordered Drake to make another "descent on the Indies"—that is, another voyage to the Caribbean for plunder and profit. Elizabeth named Drake and Sir John Hawkins as co-commanders of a

Sir Francis Drake, "daring navigator and prince of corsairs"

fleet of 6 royal warships and 21 well-armed merchant ships, carrying about 1,500 seamen and 1,000 soldiers. Their fleet cleared Plymouth in early September.

News reached the two kinsmen that a Spanish galleon loaded with treasure had run aground at San Juan, Puerto Rico. As might be expected, they headed for San Juan. But Hawkins was not well and died of dysentery—an acute intestinal disorder—within sight of the island. Drake attacked the island on November 23 and 24, but found it too heavily defended. He backed off and sailed for the Spanish Main. Drake and his marauders sacked Nombre de Dios and other places on the mainland, but found little of value.

With hopes for great riches fading fast, the fleet made for Porto-belo, a seaport village on the Caribbean coast of Panama, and unknown ports beyond. Drake told Thomas Maynarde, a captain of soldiers aboard his ship, "God hath many things in store for us, and I knowe many meanes to do her majestie good service, and to make us ritch."

En route to Portobelo, Drake himself contracted dysentery and died "like a soldier" on February 7, 1596. According to a 1652 account, he was buried at sea.

> *"His corps[e] being laid into a Cophin of Lead, he was let downe into the Sea, the Trumpets in dolefull manner echoing out this lamentation for so great a losse, and all the Cannons in the fleet were discharged according to the custome of all Sea Funeral obsequies* [rites]."

Loved at home and feared in the rest of the world, Drake opened new vistas to his tiny island nation. After he circled the globe, England built an empire upon which the sun never set. More than four hundred years after the death of Sir Francis Drake—daring navigator and prince of corsairs—his legend still resonates like a cannon's roar through the corridors of time.

Sir Francis Drake and His Times

1538–1545 Frances Drake born at Crowndale, Devon, England.

1566 Accompanies John Lovell on slaving voyage to the New World.

1567 Commands fifty-ton *Judith* on John Hawkins's third slave-trading voyage; Hawkins and Drake narrowly survive sea battle with Spanish fleet off coast of Veracruz, Mexico.

1570–1572 Plunders Spanish ships and settlements during three successful voyages to Caribbean; leads daring land attack on Nombre de Dios; crosses Isthmus of Panama and intercepts Spanish mule trains bearing silver.

1577 Embarks on around-the-world voyage from Plymouth, England, with five ships.

1579 Lands in California and claims land for England as "Nova Albion."

1580 Completes circumnavigation of globe with one ship, the *Golden Hind*.

1581 Elizabeth I knights Drake.

1585–1586 Captains expedition to West Indies; raids Santo Domingo and Cartagena.

1587 Attacks ships assembling in Cádiz for Spanish Armada.

1588 Plays important role in disrupting and routing Spanish Armada.

1595 Sails on last expedition to West Indies.

1596 Drake dies of dysentery at sea near Portobelo, Panama.

Further Research

Books

Atlas of Exploration. New York: Farrar Straus and Giroux, 1988.

Bedini, Silvio A., et al., eds. *Christopher Columbus and the Age of Exploration: An Encyclopedia*. New York: Da Capo, 1998.

Corn, Charles. *The Scents of Eden: A History of the Spice Trade.* New York: Kodansha International, 1999.

Durant, Will and Ariel. *The Age of Reason Begins: A History of European Civilization in the Period of Shakespeare, Bacon, Montaigne, Rembrandt, Galileo, and Descartes: 1558–1648.* The Story of Civilization, vol. 7. New York: Simon & Schuster, 1961.

Gerrard, Roy. *Sir Francis Drake: His Daring Deeds.* New York: Farrar Straus and Giroux, 1988.

Guy, J. A. *Drake and the 16th-Century Explorers*. Great Explorer series. Hauppage, New York: Barron's, 1998.

The Drake Manuscript in the Pierpont Morgan Library. London: André Deutsch, 1996.

Novaresio, Paolo. *The Explorers: From the Ancient World to the Present.* New York: Stewart, Tabori & Chang, 1996.

Websites

Sir Francis Drake
   http://www.marinhistory.org/articles/drake.htm

Sir Francis Drake's Famous Voyage Round the World, 1580
   http://www.fordham.edu/halsall/mod/1580Pretty-drake.html

Francis Drake
   http://www.mariner.org/age/drake.html

Further Research

Pirates and Privateers - Sir Francis Drake
   http: //legends.dm.net/pirates/drake.html

Sir Francis Drake
   http: //www.mcn.org/2/oseeler/drake.htm

BIBLIOGRAPHY

Books

Bohlander, Richard E., ed. *World Explorers and Discoverers*. New York: Da Capo Press, 1998.

Boorstin, Daniel J. *The Discoverers*. New York: Random House, 1983.

Brinkley, Douglas. *American Heritage History of the United States*. New York: Viking, 1998.

Cordingly, David. *Under the Black Flag: The Romance and the Reality of Life Among the Pirates*. New York: Random House, 1995.

Cordingly, David, ed. *Pirates: Terror on the High Seas, from the Caribbean to the South China Sea*. Atlanta: Turner Publishing, 1996.

Cordingly, David, and John Falconer. *Pirates Fact & Fiction*. New York: Cross River Press, 1992.

Duncan, Alice Smith. *Sir Francis Drake and the Struggle for an Ocean Empire*. World Explorers series. New York: Chelsea House, 1993.

Dupuy, R. Ernest, and Trevor N. Dupuy. *The Encyclopedia of Military History from 3500 B.C. to the Present*. Rev. ed. New York: Harper & Row, 1977.

Fischer, David Hackett. *The Great Wave: Price Revolutions and the Rhythm of History*. New York: Oxford University Press, 1996.

Fuller, J. F. C. *A Military History of the Western World, Volume II: From the Defeat of the Spanish Armada to the Battle of Waterloo*. New York: Da Capo Press, 1987.

Gallagher, Jim. *Sir Francis Drake and the Foundation of a World Empire*. Explorers of New Worlds series. Philadelphia: Chelsea House, 2001.

Hakluyt, Richard. *Voyages and Discoveries: The Principal Navigations, Voyages, Traffiques and Discoveries of the English Nation*. Edited, abridged, and introduced by Jack Beeching. New York: Penguin Books, 1985.

Hogg, Ian V. *The Hutchinson Dictionary of Battles*. Oxford, England: Helicon Publishing, 1998.

Bibliography

Kelsey, Harry. *Sir Francis Drake: The Queen's Pirate.* New Haven, CT: Yale University Press, 1998.

Kemp, Peter, ed. *The Oxford Companion to Ships and the Sea.* New York: Oxford University Press, 1988.

King, Dean, with John B. Hattendorf and J. Worth Estes. *A Sea of Words: A Lexicon and Companion for Patrick O'Brian's Seafaring Tales.* 2d ed. New York: Henry Holt, 1997.

King, Dean, with John B. Hattendorf. *Harbors and High Seas: An Atlas and Geographical Guide to the Aubrey-Maturin Novels of Patrick O'Brian.* New York: Henry Holt, 1996.

Laffin, John. *Brassey's Dictionary of Battles: 3,500 Years of Conflict, Campaigns, and Wars.* New York: Barnes & Noble, 1998.

Marrin, Albert. *The Sea King: Sir Francis Drake and His Times.* New York: Atheneum Books for Young Readers, 1995.

Marx, Jenifer. *Pirates and Privateers of the Caribbean.* Malabar, FL: Krieger Publishing, 1992.

Reader, John. *Africa: A Biography of the Continent.* New York: Alfred A. Knopf, 1998.

Rogozinski, Jan. *Pirates!: Brigands, Buccaneers, and Privateers in Fact, Fiction, and Legend.* New York: Da Capo Press, 1996.

Sherry, Frank. *Pacific Passions: The European Struggle for Power in the Great Ocean in the Age of Exploration.* New York: William Morrow, 1994.

Stanley, Jo, ed. *Bold in Her Breeches: Women Pirates Across the Ages.* London; San Francisco: Pandora, 1995.

Thomas, Hugh. *The Slave Trade: The Story of the Atlantic Slave Trade, 1440–1870.* New York: Simon & Schuster, 1997.

Whiting, John Roger Scott. *The Enterprise of England: The Spanish Armada.* New York: St. Martin's Press, 1988.

Williams, Glyndwr. *The Great South Sea: English Voyages and Encounters, 1570–1750.* New Haven, CT: Yale University Press, 1997.

Bibliography

Articles

Cummins, John. "That Golden Knight: Drake and His Reputation." *History Today* [Great Britain]. 1996, 46 (1), pp. 14–21.

Pierson, Peter. "Elizabeth's Pirate Admiral." *MHQ: The Quarterly Journal of Military History.* 1996, 8 (4), pp. 80–91.

Winchester, Simon. "Sir Francis Drake Is Still Capable of Kicking Up a Fuss." *Smithsonian.* 1997, 27 (10), pp. 82–88, 90–91.

Source Notes

Chapter 1:

Pg. 8: "Francis Drake, by the best estimate": Harry Kelsey, *Sir Francis Drake: The Queen's Pirate.* (Yale University Press, 1998), p. 7.

Pg. 11: "enemies of God": Albert Marrin, *The Sea King: Sir Francis Drake and His Times.* (Atheneum, 1995), p. 9

Pg. 11: "a pretty sum": Ibid., p. 10.

Pg. 12: "a cheerful expression": Alice Smith Duncan, *Sir Francis Drake and the Struggle for an Ocean Empire.* (Chelsea House, 1993), p. 27.

Pg. 13: "our Negroes": Marrin, p. 16.

Chapter 2:

Pg. 20: "We coasted from place to place": David Cordingly, *Under the Black Flag: The Romance and the Reality of Life Among the Pirates.* (Random House, 1995), p. 38.

Pg. 22: "giving him to understand": Duncan, p. 32.

Pg. 23: "The Judith forsooke us": Kelsey, p. 39.

Pg. 23: "the defining moment": Peter Pierson, "Elizabeth's Pirate Admiral". (MHQ: The Quarterly Journal of Military History, 1996, 8 (4)), pp. 80–91.

Chapter 3:

Pg. 26: "to gaine such intelligences": Duncan, p. 36.

Pgs. 28–29: "are well disposed": Ibid, p. 38.

Pg. 29: "two [cimarrones] would carry": Marrin, p. 46.

Pg. 29: "upon the coast of Nombre de Diós": David F. Marley, "The Lure of Spanish Gold," in *Pirates: Terror on the High Seas, from the Caribbean to the South China Sea.* (Turner Publishing, 1996), p. 30.

Pg. 30: "the treasure house": Jim Gallagher, *Sir Francis Drake and the Foundation of a World Empire.* Explorers of the Worlds series. (Chelsea House, 2001), p. 26.

Pg. 30: "verie loving friend": Jennifer Marx, *Pirates and Privateers of the Caribbean.* (Krieger Publishing, 1992), p. 71.

Pg. 30: "Captain Drake, if you fortune to come": Ibid.

Pg. 31: "Almighty God": Marrin, p. 47.

Chapter 4:

Pg. 36: "He furnished at his own propper charge": Kelsey, p. 71.

Pg. 36: "I would gladly be revenged": Duncan, p. 52.

Pg. 37: "Between men of war and mariners": Kelsey, p. 85.

Pgs. 40–41: "In this port our General": Sir Francis Drake's Famous Voyage Round the World, 1580, p. 5, http://www.fordham.edu/halsall/mod/1580Pretty-drake.html

Pg. 41: "This is the end": Kelsey, p. 109.

Pg. 42: God seemed to set Himself": Marrin, p.64.

Pg. 43: "one and the self same sea": Duncan, pg. 66.

Pgs. 44–45: "called this country Nova Albion": Sir Francis Drake's Famous Voyage Round the World, 1580, p. 12.

Pg. 45: "her majesty's right and title": Ibid.

Pg. 46: "laid up fast upon a desperate shoal": Duncan, pp. 83–84.

Chapter 5:

Pg. 47: "Be the queen alive and well": Marrin, p. 78.

Pg. 48: "the master thief": Gallagher, p. 11.

Pg. 48: "the plunders committed": Marx, p. 82.

Pg. 51: "beyond the line": Ibid., p. 83.

Pg. 52: "descent of the Indies": Peter Kemp, ed. *The Oxford Companion to Ships and the Sea.* (Oxford University Press, 1988), p. 265.

Pg. 52: "And albeit for divers days together": Marx, pp. 83–84.

Chapter 6:

Pg. 54: "put fire into their house": Pierson, p. 85.

Pg. 54: "Enterprise of England": Roger Whiting. The Enterprise of England: The Spanish Armada. (St. Martin's Press, 1988), p. 7.

Pg. 56: "It hath pleased God": Kelsey, p. 297.

Pg. 56: "he had singed the king": Duncan, p. 94.

Pg. 56: "Prepare in England strongly": Ibid.

Pg. 58: "There is plenty of time": Simon Winchester. "Sir Francis Drake is Still Capable of Kicking up a Fuss," *Smithsonian*, 1997, 27 (10), p. 83.

Pg. 62: "to make him spend the best blood": Pierson, p. 88.

Pg. 62: "the devil ships are coming": Marrin, p. 127.

Pg. 62: "I have read it all": Duncan, p. 100.

Afterword:

Pg. 64: "a daring navigator and a prince of corsairs": Pierson, p. 80.

Pg. 66: "God hath many things in store": Kelsey, p. 388.

Pg. 66: "like a soldier": Pierson, p. 91.

Pg. 66: "His corps[e] being laid into a Cophin of Lead": Kelsey, pp. 390–91.

Index

Page numbers in **boldface** are illustrations.